A Time Called Tullibody

Boyhood in a Post-War Village

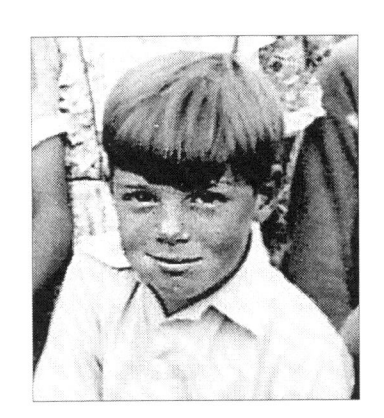

Drew Jamieson

Copyright © 2020 Drew Jamieson

All rights reserved.

ISBN: 9798642658253

Independently published

By the same Author

The Ochil Hills: A Special Place (2018)
Where the Wild Trout Swim (2018)
Where the Wild Salmon Run (2018)
A Scottish Angler's Companions (2018)
Trout from Scottish Reservoirs (2019)
The Trout Reservoirs of Lothian (2019)
Scotland's Wild Salmon (2019)
Fishing and Flying (2020)

Available on amazon.co.uk.

Front Cover: The 'Woodside Gang' - Woodside Terrace c 1949

DEDICATION

To Morny,
my wife and soulmate.

ACKNOWLEDGEMENTS

"Nothing is impossible - if you don't have to do it yourself." - is a well-worn maxim and only too true. No book starts by itself. There has to be an impetus. Every author needs motivation to put the first word on a blank page and there needs to be a story worth putting on that blank page.

That story, the material of this book - the childhood memories and many of the photographs - I owe to my Mum and my Dad, my Gran and my Grandad, my Uncle Willie Dallas and all my friends of these Tullibody years. Some of the photographs are my own, many historic ones were captured by lens-men and lens-women unknown and long gone. I acknowledge their contribution to this book.

The motivation I credit to the Tullibody History Group - in particular to Christine Calder and Ian Allan. The original draft had been written for the interest of my own family but Chris and Ian thought that it might interest a wider readership. The judgement is yours.

CONTENTS

Before The Beginning   1

Tullibody   3

The Roads To Tullibody   9

The Street of the Ochils   23

The Terrace Beside the Woods   37

The Brae at the Baingle   57

Further Horizons   69

Further Enjoyment   91

TIME

One 'Theory of Time', suggests that historic events exist in a series of circles, which may revolve in different directions and at different speeds but which, every so often, coincide and 'Times Past' surface in the 'Present'. I am not saying that I fully adhere to that theory but, every so often, some strange combination of circumstances suggests some form of 'deja vu'.

However, this story is not about 'circular time'. For myself, life seems to be defined by different times and different places - a 'Glasgow' time; a 'Germany' time; an 'Edinburgh' time; a 'Stirling' time - but all these later 'times' started with:-

"A Time Called Tullibody"

BEFORE THE BEGINNING

".. and the sights and thoughts of my youth pursue me; and I see like a vision the youth of my father, and of his father, and the whole stream of lives flowing down there far in the north, with the sound of laughter and tears, to cast me out in the end, as by a sudden freshet, on these ultimate islands. And I admire and bow my head before the romance of destiny."

Robert Louis Stevenson

When my father and mother died I found photograph albums full of images of far-away places and long-ago people. Every image held a story but I was too late to unlock the stories because Mum and Dad had gone and hadn't told the story which would bring the images to life and link them together in some sort of narrative. I thought it very sad. Dad left so little and had died so early in my life that I had to do a lot of research to piece together his story. Mum told me more of her story before she died and left lots of photographs.

I was born in Glasgow, just off the Maryhill Road, in 1940, during the Second World War and just before the Clydebank blitz. In those days Mum would take us out of Glasgow as often as possible to her parents - my Gran and Grandad - in Tullibody, for safety. So I first visited Tullibody at a very early age. We finally left Glasgow for Tullibody in 1948 to enable Mum to look after Gran after an operation.

So looking at my own photographs and notebooks it seemed worthwhile to try to put them all in some kind of context. I had put the most significant photographs into a series of photo-books but these contain no words, no story. So the purpose of this book is to join up the pictures and share the stories before they are forgotten.

Drew Jamieson
Stirling
2020

Drew Jamieson

…..And I saw in the turning so clearly a child's
Forgotten mornings when he walked with his mother
Through the parables
Of sunlight
And the legends of green chapels

From *"Poem in October"* by Dylan Thomas

TULLIBODY

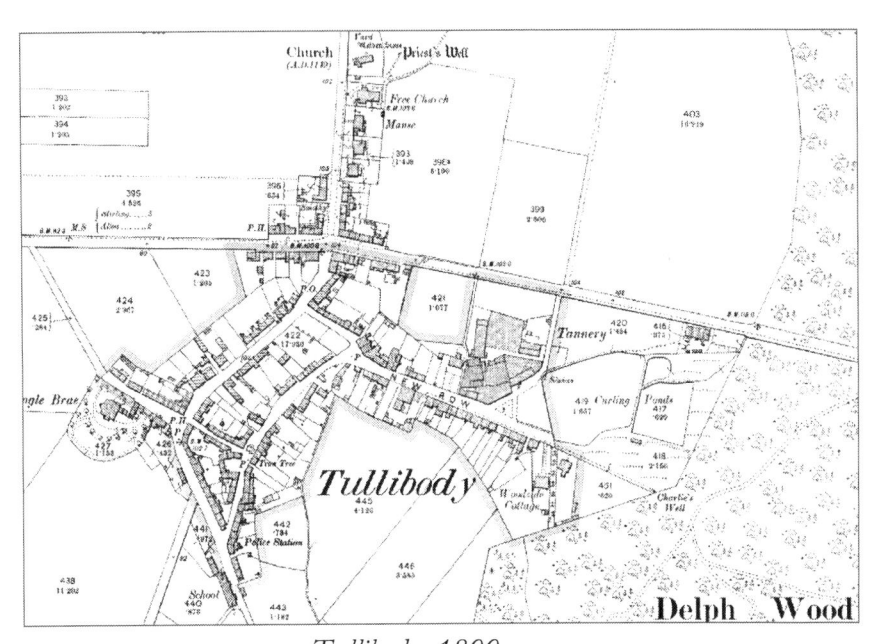

Tullibody c1899
'Reproduced with the permission of the National Library of Scotland'

Tullibody is described, prosaically, in Wikipedia, as: *"a town set in the Central Lowlands of Scotland. It lies north of the River Forth near to the foot of the Ochil Hills within the Forth Valley. The town is 1.8 miles (2.9 km) south-west of Alva, 1.8 miles (2.9 km) north-west of Alloa and 4.0 miles (6.4 km) east-northeast of Stirling."*

But Tullibody is much more than that. Tullibody is reputed to be one of the oldest villages in Scotland. There is evidence of early peoples living in the area and worshipping the sun. It is believed that the stone in Tullibody War Memorial formed part of a Druid Circle. These early people hunted and gathered food from the land and sea when Tullibody looked very different - a peninsula, surrounded by water. A shell midden was found, containing the remains of mussels, scallops and cockles dating back to around 4000BC.

The Romans were in the area during the first few centuries AD and there is a suggestion of a Roman camp and a ford across the Forth at Manor Powis. St Serf is believed to have set up a church on the site of the present Auld Kirk in the 5th century when Christianity was brought over from Ireland. Kenneth McAlpine, King of Scots, is reputed to have amassed his army on Baingle Brae before he fought and subdued the Picts. There was a standing stone on the main road to Stirling until the early 1900s.

David 1 of Scotland was responsible for Tullibody's claim to fame when in 1149 he granted the lands and fishing rights in the River Forth to Cambuskenneth Abbey. It was then that the Auld Kirk was erected, where it still stands today. Tullibody has been served well, being the Parish Church until that time when it lost its celebrity status and Alloa took the title. The Abercrombys made the Auld Kirk their family vault.

Tullibody Auld Kirk

There is a story that Edward 1, in his attempt to subdue the Scots in 1306, tried to build a castle in Tullibody. This might have been on the hill behind the Delph Pond but it has never been confirmed.

The lands of Tullibody have been owned by wealthy landowners for centuries. The last being the Abercrombys. The Hays were around in 1368 and Egida Hay of Tullibody married Alexander Seton of Touch, Cambusbarron in the 1400s. The original village was a small hamlet around the Auld Kirk. George Abercromby moved the hamlet across the road, to the south, in the early 1800s because the houses were in a deplorable state. Alexander Paterson commenced tanning and shoe making and so the Tannery evolved. This was later carried on by the Tullis family. The village of Cambus, down where the River Devon meets the River Forth, is part of the parish of Tullibody and Cambus. It was once a very busy port with coal being delivered to other towns. It also had three mills, including a saw mill and a flour mill. The Knox family commenced the brewing industry. The Moubrays started the distillery.

Post-War Tullibody

It is difficult to imagine, in this consumer-driven and digital 21st Century, just what post-war Scotland was like. The Second World War ran from 1939 to 1945. Born only in 1940, of course, my growing awareness of the world around me was that this was 'normal'. I knew no other. I expected the food I was given and the clothes and toys that appeared. That was normal. It is not until we have the benefit of hindsight - and the comparison with life in 2019 - that the profound difference can be appreciated.

During and after the war, food and most other essentials were 'on ration' or otherwise in very short supply. There was a long period of austerity. Rationing continued long after the war. Furniture and clothing, if you could get them, was of the 'Utility' brand - not quite Gucci. Sweets did not come 'off ration' until around 1950. Fruit and vegetables were limited unless, like Grandad, you had your own garden or an allotment and were 'Digging for Victory'. Bananas did not arrive until 1948.

There were no supermarkets. Local shops did their best with limited supplies and the local Coop was a lifeline. I had to remember my Gran's 'dividend number' - 3563 and my Mum's - 1478, when I went for the 'messages'. Milk was delivered by horse and cart. Baker and other vans came to the doors. Baking, if you could get flour, sugar and eggs, kept families alive. Clothes were made at home or were hand-me-downs from at least one generation ago. Knitting and sewing were essential skills. Most of our toys, if we had any, were home-made or hand-me-downs - or we used our imagination. No Xbox, no computer games. My first bicycle had three previous owners within our extended family.

Disease was an ever present threat to our childhood. There was no NHS until 1948. Antibiotics were scarce. For children, the government provided bottles of concentrated orange juice, rose-hip syrup and cod-liver oil for vitamins and nutrients. Rickets and polio were always a threat. Typhoid and cholera were never very far way. Children ran the gamut of measles, diphtheria, scarlet fever and mumps. Head-lice and impetigo were common.

There was no television until 1953 when a few tiny black-and-white screens showed the Coronation. Evening entertainment was listening to the 'wireless', playing board-games like 'Ludo' or 'Snakes and Ladders', card-games, reading or just talking and story-telling. There were no computers, no mobile phones. Telephones were rare. Only birds made Tweets and Twittered. Facebook was a knock on your friend's door. Google was the local library if you could get there. There were few cars. Buses cost money. You walked or ran until you had a bike - then you could travel further.

Society, in the immediate post-war period, was different too. Many men did not return or returned with injuries or conditions which limited their role in post-war life. There were many more single-parent households - coping without fathers. Different voices appeared in the village - from Poland, Latvia and Lanarkshire. There was an urgency to get the economy up and running again, with ambitious plans for local coal-mining with an expanded population and housing.

The contrast with life in 2019 is stark - until coronavirus arrived in 2020 - and the future is once again less certain.

Drew Jamieson

THE ROADS TO TULLIBODY

THE ROADS TO TULLIBODY

*"A map is not for telling you where to go.
What it tells you is exactly where you are.
You have to decide your own destination and journey."*

The Road to Tullibody - The Cross c. 1920s

In starting to write this memoir, I am reminded of Robert Louis Stevenson's emphasis on the romance of past generations - the time before "ME". He reaches back to: *"the youth of my father, and of his father, and the whole stream of lives flowing down there far in the north….."* - and I am very conscious of my own story being built upon the lives of my Mum and Dad and the histories of Gran and Grandad and older generations down the line.

I did not arrive in Tullibody by chance. First, my mother had to meet my father. Then my father had to marry my mother. Sometime after that - there was me. But long before then, my father's father had to meet my father's mother and the same for my mother's parents - and so it goes on back into the deep wells of family history. They all travelled their own roads to Tullibody. One side of the family - Mother's side, the Dallases, came from the north-east of Scotland - from Buchan, Deeside and the Mearns. Dad's side of the family came from the west and south-west - from Ayrshire and Galloway. Somehow, all their individual roads came together in Tullibody.

Going further back, using the "Scotland's People" website, the histories of the Jamieson, Kennedy, Dallas and the Donald families have been traced as far back as the late 1700s. But the back-story does not end there. Scotland's DNA tells me that, on both the Fatherline and the Motherline, my roots go back to the early pioneers who moved into Scotland after the last Ice Age. My Fatherline is defined as "Caledonian 165" and is connected to a small Pictish line currently well-represented in the West of Scotland and Ulster - no doubt the Jamieson/Kennedy grandparents. My Motherline is defined as "Mashriq" another early pioneer group with connections to the Western Isles and Grampian - no doubt the Donald/Dallas grandparents.

The Road from Ayrshire

Jamiesons have been in Ayrshire since, at least, 1693. My direct ancestors start in 1763, when Allan Jamieson, a farmer and spirit-dealer was born. He married Margaret Stevenson and had two sons, including Hugh. Hugh married Margaret Cockburn and had one son, Robert. Robert Jamieson left home to marry Ann Ralston in 1857 and went on to have six children, including Andrew, born in 1864. Robert, died, as a handloom weaver, in 1871. Andrew became my paternal Grandfather.

The Kennedy clan is traditionally based in south Ayrshire and Galloway but Kennedys have been in Beith since, at least, 1703. My first direct ancestor, a John Kennedy, was a handloom weaver born around 1790. He married Helen Knox and their son, the next John Kennedy, was born in 1813. This John Kennedy was also a weaver and married Janet Jamieson in 1833. They had five children, including the next John Kennedy. This John Kennedy married Isabella Orr in 1859 and had five children, including Janet. In 1888 Janet Kennedy married Andrew Jamieson and became my paternal Grandmother.

In 1911, the Jamiesons were living in Alloa Road, Tullibody, just east of the Cross, backing onto the Victorian villas of Menstrie Road, close to where Nicol's shop used to be and where Ochil Court is now. Some time after 1911, the family moved to Glasgow, leaving Annie, (16), in domestic service in Alva.

Andrew died in Glasgow in 1918. Janet survived until 1936. I never met them as they died before I was born. They are both buried in Tullibody cemetery.

Robert Jamieson Family (Circa 1902)
Janet (ms Kennedy)(1867-1936); John (1896-1963); Mary (1900-1909); Annie (1894-1963); Isabella (1898-1964); Andrew (1864-1918)

Robert Jamieson - My Dad

Dad with the Bibby Line c. 1930

Robert Jamieson, was born in Falkirk in 1903 and by 1911 was living in Alloa Road, Tullibody. As an 8-year-old he would also have attended Tullibody School until he moved to Glasgow. He served his engineering apprenticeship with Harland and Wolff and joined the Merchant Navy, as a marine engineer in 1927. Dad went to sea with the Lamport and Holt Line in the *MV Leighton* to South America. In 1930 he transferred to the Bibby Line and stayed there until the end of his seafaring career, much of it on troopships like the *MV Lancashire*, out and back to the Far East.

Lamport and Holt Line - MV Leighton

Bibby Line - MV Lancashire

The Road from the Mearns

The Dallas family name originated in the parish of Dallas in Morayshire, and Dallas baptisms do not appear in Kincardineshire until 1740. My direct family history in Stonehaven can be traced to a William Dallas probably as far back as 1786. William Dallas, appears in the record first in 1810, as a sawyer, and father of Isabella Dallas, daughter of Anne Kenneth. William went on to father three more children with Anne Kenneth, including William in 1820. In 1845, this William Dallas married Isabel Mitchell and had three children, including another William. In 1881, this William, working as a cooper, married Ann Adam and had seven children, including Robert Adam Dallas - who became my Granddad. While growing up in Stonehaven Robert met Ann Donald who was to become my Gran.

Donalds had been in Banffshire since the mid-1600s. My great-grandfather, George Donald was born in Macduff, in 1843, to Robert Donald, a journeyman gardener, and Ann Donald (ms Lyall). In 1861, George married Elisa Kirkton and moved to Aboyne, on Deeside. Their son, William was born in 1877 but his mother, Elisa, died in 1885. In 1887, George re-married 23-year old Mary E McHardy of Tullich, near Ballater and went on to have nine children, including my grandmother - Ann Donald. About 1900 the family left Aboyne and, no doubt following the infamous 'Slug Road' from Banchory, settled in the village of Cowie near Stonehaven. Here, Ann grew up and met Robert Dallas, who was to become my Grandad.

Around 1911, 24-year old Robert Adam Dallas, now a tanner, left Stonehaven and moved to Tullibody, initially boarding with the Reid family in the Old School House. He returned to Stonehaven to marry Ann Donald that same year and moved permanently to Tullibody. They set up house in 23 Ochil Street and adopted a niece, two-year-old Annie Dallas. Their own daughter Mary, my Mum, was born in 1912 and their son William was born in 1918.

Mary, Robert, Ann and Willie Dallas c 1923

*The Dallas Family (Ochil Street - Circa 1926)
Clockwise: Grandad, Mum, Bill Dallas (brother of Robert), Annie Dallas, Gran, Willie and Nell Dallas (sister of Robert)*

Mary Dallas - My Mum

Mary Dallas

Mary Dallas was a Tullibody girl and a country girl at heart all her life. She was born in Ochil Street in 1912, sister to (adopted) Annie, born in 1909, and to Willie, born in 1918. She went to Tullibody School and Alloa Academy and joined Paton and Baldwin's factory in Alloa.

She married in Tullibody, lived most of her life in Tullibody and died in Tullibody. Her brief sojourn in Glasgow from 1940 to 1948 was punctuated with as many visits back to Tullibody as possible. When we lived in Glasgow, Mum would take my sister Ann and I, together with our picnic stuff and spirit stove, out to the green and leafy valley of the Allander Water at Milngavie. What a contrast from the grey, grim tenements and grubby back-courts of Maryhill. Here we could breathe fresh air, run on green grass and paddle in the clear water of the Allander and from time to time see the flash or shadow of a small trout race up or down the pool.

Tullibody School c.1923
Mary Dallas, Second Row, far left

Tullibody School, 1924
Mary Dallas, Second Row, far left

Paton and Baldwins Warehouse Despatch Department 1933
Mary Dallas, Back Row, third from left.

Early motoring with friends - Sheriffmuir, 1930s

The Roads come Together

The Jamieson and the Dallas families must have had quite a bit of interaction in those early years. Andrew Jamieson and Robert Dallas would have worked in the Tannery for a number of years together. When the Jamieson's moved to Glasgow, Annie Jamieson stayed behind and took lodgings with Gran and Grandad in Ochil Street. After moving to Glasgow, Andrew, Isa, Robert and Annie all came back frequently to visit Gran in Tullibody.

Robert Jamieson returned frequently to Tullibody throughout the 1930s and married Mary Dallas in 1936.

Mum and Dad wedding - 1936

They set up house in 42 Delph Road and my sister Ann Kennedy Jamieson was born in 1937. The family moved to Glasgow in 1940 where I, Andrew Dallas Jamieson, was born in 1940.

Jean Robertson welcomes Ann to Tullibody in 1937

By the time I was born, the Dallas family was well-established in Tullibody and I was welcomed into a loving and well-respected family.

My first introduction to Tullibody, with Mum and sister, Ann.

This is my story.

THE STREET OF THE OCHILS

Drew Jamieson

OCHIL STREET

"The night is quiet, very quiet. As quiet as only a rural village at midnight can be. Suddenly, from out of the silence, comes the voice of an owl. A long, low quavering call, echoing through the darkness and shadows in the bedroom of 23 Ochil Street. I snuggle down and pull the blankets over my head to keep the "baddies" out. I am 3 years old."

Ochil Street. c1900

In the fourth year of the Second World War I was three years old. Mum had, from time to time, taken my sister, Ann, and I off to stay with her mother and father - my Gran and Grandad - in Tullibody. In those days we stayed at 23 Ochil Street. Tullibody, at that time, was indeed a small village and Ochil Street was pretty much in the centre of the old village as it was in those days. Gran's traditional "weaver's style" cottage on the east side of Ochil Street, backed on to Main Street, out the gate at the end of the back garden. I have no idea where we slept in those days. It was not a big cottage, only a 'but and ben'. I think I had a camp bed. I remember waking in the night, hearing the strike of the grandfather clock at the top of the hour and, if the night was quiet, the distant hoot of a tawny owl and, even more romantic, the distant whistle of the train approaching Cambus Station on its way from Stirling to Perth.

Ochil Street was well-named. Look between the bungalows and you could see Dumyat, we thought it was an ancient volcano, dominating the northern horizon. Look up the street and you could see the broad slopes of Ben Cleuch, often carrying its wreath of snow - the Maiden's or Lady's Veil - well into springtime days. The Ochil Hills were ever-present.

In my Gran's house there was an outside wash-house with large wooden tubs. In one of the wooden tubs Grandad had put a shoal of 'pinheads' - tiny, silver young sticklebacks. Grandad did not need any excuse to show me where the 'pinheads' came from. A short walk out the back gate, past Mrs Edmonstone's garden, on to Main Street, past the house bearing the plaque honouring Robert Dick, the famous geologist, up Delph Road past the Tannery, to an apparently vast expanse of water - the Delph Pond.

Grandad

Grandad came to Tullibody as a tanner and remained a tanner all his life. Some form of tannery had been in Tullibody since 1806. In the small village that Tullibody was then, where the Tannery was the major employer, Grandad had a large circle of friends and workmates in the village. He was also active in local football. Having played for Cowie FC (Stonehaven) in his youth, he helped coach the Tullibody FC team as young man.

By the time I came along, Grandad knew everybody in Tullibody. Well everyone worth knowing and he opened doors throughout my childhood. Grandad pulled a favour with Geordie, the gamekeeper. He knew the milkman and his horse and I got to ride the milk cart in the mornings. When I wanted an aviary, he knew the man that bred budgies. When I wanted to build a canoe, he knew the joiner that made canoes. He knew all the right folk for a small boy, did Grandad.

Tullibody FC - pre-1914
R Dallas, J Robertson, J Dickson, T Keir, J Blair
A Morrison, Blair, R Paterson, J Ferguson, Unknown, Unknown, J Millar, M Rennie D Bain, Unknown, Unknown, W Millar, D Buick, M Heir, R Millar Snr

The Tannery

The Tannery had dominated the economy and culture of Tullibody since the Paterson family extended their original tannery and bone works in 1806. By the 1840s the Tullibody tannery had 30 to 40 employees. By 1890 the business was owned by *"John Tullis & Son, Leather Manufacturer"*, based in Glasgow and by 1951, there were about 85 workers - of which Grandad was one. Throughout most of that time, the community was regulated by the "hooter" declaring the start and finish of the working day and the midday break. It gave a defined odour to many parts of the village.

The Tannery c 1920

In later years I would understand the work that Grandad did as a tanner. Going to and from school, I look through an open door at the Tannery for a few minutes watching him work:

"He wears a full-length leather apron and bends over a long curved table which slopes at a steep angle towards the floor. He uses a long curved knife, with handles at both ends, to scrape hair and flesh from the animal hide stretched across the curved table. When this hide is finished, he hooks the next hide from a floor-pit of noxious liquid and starts again - bend, scrape, bend, scrape. The rest of the Tannery is dark, noisy and smelly. Wheels, cogs and belts rattle overhead. Voices echo across the space. The floor consists of multiple pits of toxic and smelly liquids filled with animal hides. " - It was a small boy's vision of Hell.

Grandad continued to work in the tannery until he retired in 1952. He and Gran moved to Woodside Terrace, Alloa Road in the early 1940s, where they stayed until Gran died in 1960. Grandad came to stay with Mum, at Baingle Brae until he died in 1963.

Gran

If Grandad was the breadwinner, Gran was the homemaker. My memories are of the delightful smells of cooking, baking and jam-making. For much of our summer holidays the kitchen would be filled with the big copper "jeely-pan", conical sieve, rows of glass jam jars, paper lids held on with rubber bands each meticulously labelled with name of jam and date of production.

Tannery workers c.1920s

Tannery workers c. 1940s

Throughout the summer, as the weeks rolled past, the kitchen would be filled with the aromas of boiling fruit - strawberries, raspberries, blackcurrants, and, perhaps if we had been out foraging in the woods, hedges or the 'Ham and Egg Braes', there might be bramble, blaeberry or crab apple jelly.

Picnic - Gran and friends

Picnic with the Robertsons - Menstrie Glen 1923

When Gran wasn't making jam she was baking. The house was never without staples like scones, shortbread, pancakes, fruit loaf or Empire biscuits. For treats there were sponges - Victoria sponge with jam in the middle, chocolate sponge, sponges with butter-icing, coffee-icing and, occasionally, walnut. The baking and jam was not all for our household. Gran was always baking for someone or something else - the Church sale-of-work, the Red Cross bazaar, the Bowling Club or a Whist Drive. Anywhere serving teas needed baking. Anything needing fund-raising, needed jam and sponges. I often wondered, with hindsight, where all the sugar came from, in that time of post-war rationing, but I suspect it was pooled from various friends and neighbours to whom some of the finished jam, jelly or baking would be returned pro-rata.

Both Gran and Grandad were "weel-kent" throughout the village. They were active in the Bowling Club at Cambus, they supported Reverend Rose in St Serf's Church and Gran was very involved in the Red Cross. They had a lifelong friendship with the Robertsons of Banchory Place and the Fletchers of Cambus. Picnics were great social events in those days and the photograph album records some of them. Menstrie Glen and Sheriffmuir were favourite destinations in the 1920s and 1930s.

Sometime in that era Gran must have had some connection with the Forresters of Tullibody House - but I know not what? There are photographs in the album of the governess and two of the Forrester children at some riverbank where Gran must have taken the photograph. There may have been a connection through the Clackmannan and Kinross Branch of the British Red Cross Society where Gran was particularly active during both World Wars. She was later invited to the *"Presentation of Letters of Thanks to Red Cross Workers"* by Captain J C Stewart, Chairman of the Scottish Branch of the British Red Cross Society in Alloa Town Hall on 2 November 1946 and, like many of her contemporaries, qualified for the green and orange ribbon of the Defence Medal, awarded after the War.

Gran and Grandad are buried in Tullibody Old Kirkyard.

Willie Dallas - Uncle Willie

When I first came to Ochil Street, Willie Dallas was away serving during the Second World War. I must have first met him when he was home on leave because I apparently called him "Uncle Gun".

"Uncle Gun" - 3133273 Fusilier William Dallas

Willie had been born in Ochil Street in 1918, had gone to school and spent his boyhood there. After the war, Willie came home, with a few bits of shrapnel collected at Salerno, and other places, and took up his old trade of cobbler in Alloa. When we moved through to Woodside Terrace in 1949, my Dad was back at sea and Willie adopted my education in the ways of the world.

Fishing was one of Willie's interests - in more ways than one. Our first fishing experience was on a family picnic at Crook of Devon, not far above the infamous Cauldron Linn waterfall. Overreaching the water, I toppled in and, gasping and terrified, drifted rapidly down-river towards the infamous falls. Willie was the only one quick enough and strong enough to "fish" me out before too much damage was done - except to my dignity.

Tullibody Cubs at Menstrie. c. 1927
Willie Dallas, Third Row, far right.

Saturdays were Willie's day off and treats were in store. To a small boy from Tullibody a visit to Alloa was a big deal in those days and a visit to Fusco's cafe with your favourite uncle was heaven. There was quite an Italian influence in Alloa. After all, Charles Forte founded his empire from Alloa, Fusco's and Orlandi's were little bits of Italy to brighten up a Scottish climate. Marble tables and ornate skylights come to mind with vanilla ice cream covered in chocolate vermicelli or, a special treat, ice-cream sundaes with fruit and cream in a tall vase-shaped glass. For years Fusco's was a regular Saturday event as Willie met his friends or did his shopping around the town.

Willie married Sadie McDaid in 1956, lived in Alloa and worked in the Alloa Glassworks until he retired. Willie bought a car when cars were few and far between and he was my one and only driving instructor. Willie's Standard Eight was a great car to learn on long, gentle drives through almost empty roads along the Hillfoots, through Glen Devon and round the Ochil Hills. Willlie died in 1979 and is buried in Sunnyside Cemetery, Alloa.

Ann Kennedy Jamieson - 'Big Sister'

One advantage of being the second-born in a family, is that you arrive with instant company - whether you want it or not! A second advantage is that you have a 'buffer' between you and your parents. For most of my childhood my late dear sister - Ann Kennedy Jamieson - provided both of these advantages.

Looking after Little Brother

Of course, I have no memory of any time when Ann was not there. Having been born in 1937, Ann was always three-and-a-bit years older than me and was part of my normal existence from Day One. So I suspect early play was in one direction only - Ann would be tasked to amuse and look after 'little brother'. In many respects that relationship continued throughout my boyhood. Ann was always there, looking after and looking out for, little brother. No doubt if I was naughty - Ann would get the blame. Surprisingly I don't recall any fighting. If we disagreed we both just took the huff in different directions - until we needed company again.

Growing up in wartime Glasgow, we were perhaps thrown together more than usual. External friendships were limited in a big city. Air raids and wartime privations kept a family close -

and Ann was my 'minder'. Later on, it worked both ways. After the war the cinemas became more accessible. Ann desperately wanted to see the 'girlie' film *"The Red Shoes"* in one cinema but would only be allowed if I went too. I agreed but only if Ann would take me to see the cowboy *"Red River"* in another cinema the next week. Mutual support - at an early date.

Big Sister and Little Brother - Glasgow c1943

On our visits to Tullibody, Ann was always the oldest of the 'Woodside Gang' so I suspect always acted as *de facto* leader of the diverse 'patrol' of youngsters that we were. When we moved finally to Tullibody in 1948, Ann could not immediately join us. She had started senior school at North Kelvinside so was allowed to stay with relatives in Glasgow until the end of term. Thereafter we were all together again at Woodside Terrace.

THE TERRACE BESIDE THE WOODS

Drew Jamieson

WOODSIDE TERRACE

The Woodside Gang, c. 1948
Clockwise from left: Anne Grinly, Ann Jamieson, Margaret Grinly, ?, Alex McGregor, Peter Masting, Drew Jamieson, Betty Grinly, Ian Porst, Iain McGregor

Sometime before 1944, Gran and Grandad had moved house from Ochil Street to Woodside Terrace, Alloa Road. This was close to the Delph Pond and to the Tullibody Woods. It was close to the fields across the road. Initially we visited Woodside Terrace only on summer holidays from 1944 to 1948. Then in 1948 Mum had to come back from Glasgow to look after Gran and we stayed. One of the joys of Woodside Terrace was the playmates. As neighbours we had the Grinly family of three delightful sisters - Anne, Margaret and Betty.

At the end of the terrace was the McGregor family. Alex and younger brother Iain. Other faces appear in photographs - names are more difficult. Ian Porst was a young lad with a Polish father who lived in the 'Happyland', the older block of houses just east, across the fence from Gran's house. Shortly after the end of the War, the Masting family arrived from Latvia and Peter joined the gang.

Apart from the more formal picnics, summer days featured frequent tea-parties and weddings. Tea parties were easily organised. Tea-leaves were conjured up from the dried flowers of the docken plant. Crisp and dark brown just like the real thing - so long as you didn't drink it. Sugar was conjured by scraping the blocks of soft white sandstone into suitable containers for a delicate tea party. Imaginary sandwiches and scones completed the occasion.

Weddings took a little longer. Dresses in all styles and sizes seem to be stored for just such occasions and a fashion show of the very latest styles was laid on. A small boy had to be careful to avoid being roped into any official role in these weddings but it was strictly for the girls.

Woodside wedding c. 1948
Ann Jamieson, Betty Grinly, Anne Grinly, Margaret Grinly.

The Delph Pond

The Delph - from Woodside kitchen window

There is no clear evidence as to when the Delph Pond, or ponds, were created. The name, originally Delf, is from the Saxon delvan - to *delve* - to dig, and means anything dug - as a hollow or quarry. The pond has evidently been a natural hollow filled with water from the neighbouring woods. It was deepened and improved for the early tanwork, but is understood to be the common property of the village with the ground round about it being known as the 'commonry'. Two ponds appear in the earliest Ordnance Survey maps. The OS map labels them as "curling ponds". Again, were they created for that recreation or were they just used for curling because they were there?

By the time I came to the Delph Ponds in the 1940s there were definitely two ponds - the larger pond which remains today - and a smaller, rectangular pond - the Little or Wee Delph - to the east which sometimes dried out in summer. In addition there was a small reedy hollow just beyond our garden hedge, where a trickle of water flowed into the larger pond to keep it topped up.

The Delph Ponds were full of wildlife and a constant source of education and fun. The main pond supported a colony of black-headed gulls for much of the year although they did not nest there. Moorhens were resident but no coots. Summer days were filled with the high-pitched trill of the little grebes, or dabchicks, which nested most seasons. A pair of swans were regular nesters, apparently since 1936, and aggressively guarded their nest from curious small boys and especially dogs.

The traditional pair of swans

Frogs and toads were common, especially in the breeding season when the small reedy hollow rang to their croaking, day and night. Newts were a great delight - miniature dragons to our eyes - and were common in the smaller pond. The male great crested newt looked a fearsome black creature while the paler female was much more demure without the menacing crest.

But it was the fish that were the major fascination in those days. Sticklebacks, or 'baggie minnins' were the main quarry to start with. Caught with a small worm tied onto a piece of thread and kept in a jam, or 'jeely', jar. They had their own hierarchy. The colourful males in full spawning dress were stunning in an electric blue-green back and scarlet chest - known to us as 'rid-breesters' - were a popular quarry but the big trophies were the pregnant females, green and silver in colour but several times the size of the males. The largest got the acclaim as big 'sousters', would almost fill a jam jar on their own and earned bragging rights among the young anglers.

In time, and probably by accident, one day a monster fish was caught. The size of our hand, big mouth, bright orange fins, dark stripes down its sides and a fearsome spine of sharp points sticking up. We had caught a perch. Thereafter, sticklebacks were for kids. We wanted perch - and assiduously pursued them. Pocket money was spent on real pointed hooks from Alloa, along with new fangled, almost-invisible, nylon to tie them to the line. Longer bamboo poles were needed and eventually ancient long-forgotten fishing rods and reels were unearthed from damp sheds. Floats and weights were required and larger worms. The perch came in various sizes - small, medium and large - and fostered the rise of the traditional competitive spirit to catch the biggest one and the 'one that got away' - which of course grew with the telling.

The Fisherman c1946

Although the perch was the biggest trophy fish for us boys in the Delph, there were rumours of even bigger fish. Fearsome pike were supposed to lie in wait for unwary boys but, although we were there almost every day in summer, we never saw any evidence of them. No dead bodies, no disappearing ducklings, no tell-tale swirl of water from the shallows - nothing. Every so often a grown-up appeared on the banks with a stool, a proper rod and a tin of 'gi-normous' worms. These were heaved out to the middle of the Delph - it appeared to us - and the grown-up waited and waited - and didn't catch anything that we saw. But he came back again and again.

The mystery deepened. Then one day, in late autumn, on my way home from school, I chanced to look into the water just above the pipe where the trickle of water came through from the reedy hollow. It was a dull day and, at first, they looked like two logs, lying side by side, where I had never seen logs before. They were grey and mottled and looked just like the bed of the pond. Then one of the logs moved, ever so slightly and the image gradually emerged of two fish, huge fish, huge spotted fish, lying there, fins gently moving. They were trout, brown trout, big trout. There was no place for trout to spawn, either in the Delph or in the inflow trickle. There are no young trout ever seen or caught in the Delph. Perhaps this pair had been introduced by someone, perhaps the grown-up who came from time to time to fish for them? Perhaps each autumn they came to the inflow pipe to savour the sweet water which reminded them of their youth and the urges to run upstream to spawn - but cannot do so.

But the Delph was about more than wildlife and fishing. It was an adventure playground before adventure playgrounds were invented. No self-respecting pond could do without a raft or two and there were plenty of those. The older boys brought oil drums, timbers, planks of wood - anything that might or might not float - and launched them hopefully across the water. Some floated a short way. Many capsized or fell apart. A few were more successful and lasted a day or two. Rafts were OK but in a post-war world fed on stories of the 'Cockleshell Heroes' you really wanted a canoe. Without the modern fibre glass and plastic, a collapsible canoe was thought to be the answer. A framework of long stringers of wood, wrapped up in canvas sacking and covered in tar was the design but the construction was more difficult. Several different models were tried but few were successful and none were in any way safe. In summer the Delph was popular for swimming. It was relatively shallow, we estimated it at between three and six feet at the deepest and the water warmed up quickly. In winter the Delph often froze and in most winters the ice was thick enough for skating or at least walking on. When the ice was thick enough, we ventured out with sledge and skates, trying to ignore the creaking and groaning of the ice beneath us. Tullibody had a reputation as one of the oldest and best curling clubs in the area but it was a sporadic event in my time.

Geordie

Geordie's Kingdom - the Blackmuir Woods

"From the gap in the hedge at the bottom of Grandad's garden I could hear the heavy tramp of well-worn boots, the rasping breath from gassed lungs and the click of a walking stick on the gravel path. At 6 o'clock in the morning Geordie was coming. As he passed the gate I slipped in behind him and the three of us - old Geordie, his black labrador, and a small 10-year-old boy - continued in silence on our way indian-file - to the woods."

Geordie, was the local gamekeeper or 'gemmie' as known to us boys. He was a familiar, respected and even feared, controller of the woods and moors around Tullibody. Deaf as a post, stooped with age and war wounds and lungs severely damaged by gas in the trenches, Geordie was out early every morning whatever the weather. He walked a steady, measured pace, never hurried, frequent stops to look around and never spoke. He was my mentor. So much I learned about wildlife and the countryside I learned from him. He never spoke, just did his job and it all oozed in through my pores.

Geordie and Grandad had been neighbours in Ochil Street, before Grandad moved to Woodside Terrace. I had developed an interest in birds and spent my holidays combing the nearby woods, but Geordie 'keepered' the woods further away - Blackmuir Woods. Up the road and over the hill, through the oakwood up to the moor and down through the pine wood to the knackery. With Geordie I was a favour to Grandad. Initially I was just tolerated - and ignored. I was an obligement for his old friend - my Grandad. I am sure he thought I would soon get bored and one morning I would not be waiting at Grandad's gate. But he was wrong. Dark winter mornings with frost on the ground slid into spring mornings, drowning in birdsong, then summer, then autumn.

Following at the heels of Geordie we found the deep woods where the hedgehogs and foxes lived. We found the honeycombed dykes where the stoats and the weasels had their homes. We found the 'runs' where the rabbits came under the fence to graze the meadow and where the leverets lay hidden in the long grass. We found the hole where the robins nest, the mud-lined nest of the mavis, the feather-and-moss home of the 'shelfie' or chaffinch. We found the high tree nests of the carrion crow, the colonies of rooks and the rounded dome of the magpie's home. Early one morning, in some rough ground, way below the knackery on King o' Muirs road, we disturbed a wild duck - a female mallard - flapping around on the ground, trailing a wing and making much noise, trying to distract us. But

Geordie knew this trick and, bending down, lifted up a tussock of grass to reveal a cleverly-hidden nest of duck-down containing seven eggs. A privilege to see such an intimate part of the life of such a wild creatures.

It was Geordie's job, as a keeper, to protect his pheasants and, whether we approve or not, that is what he was good at. Enemies of pheasants were kept under control. I never saw him or heard him fire his shotgun in anger but foxes, stoats, weasels, crows and magpies all fell into his traps and rabbits to his snares.

One particular trick used the broken shells of hens' eggs to mimic a pheasant nest. On an open site in the moor the upturned shells were laid out to look like a clutch of pheasant eggs, visible from the sky. The nest was surrounded with birch twigs overlapping over the top such that the eggs could be seen from the air but could not be accessed from the air nor the ground - except for a narrow tunnel of twigs leading to the eggs. A crow or, more usually, a magpie would spot the eggs, come down to investigate, would soon find the access and spring the trap buried in the earth. An illegal method nowadays, for justified reasons, but it reduced the magpie population and there were more songbirds in those days.

And then other things got in the way. Whether I became a nuisance to Geordie's quiet ways or getting up before dawn lost its appeal for me but the outings became less frequent. By the time we moved from Woodside Terrace down to Baingle Brae our outings had finished. A chapter closed but the lessons learned and the enthusiasms sparked would follow me all the rest of my days.

Tullibody Woods

"The top branches of the Scots pine sway gently in the wind. The needles on the branches make a whistling noise as the wind passes through. Wood pigeons murmur softly in the darkness of the wood. An occasional clatter of wings in the branches tell of disturbance - a passing fox or sparrow hawk - scattering in alarm. The knots in the rope holding the platform together creak as the amateur construction adjusts to the swaying tree. Normally it is quiet up here, 30 feet above the ground, above the path where walkers pass beneath."

"No one looks above their head" - was the adage. Certainly for several years my tree platform was never noticed from below. This was my refuge. When I was bored, stressed, hurt or misunderstood, this was my hiding place. From this particular tree in this special place I could see to far horizons and watch the passage of massive clouds across an infinite sky. On a clear day the eye lifted across the golf course, over a line of trees and out to the shining curves and curls of the 'Links' of the River Forth. Beyond the Forth, the flat carselands stretched south to Falkirk and the great cattle markets of droving days at the Stenhouse Muir. Further south, the land rose up across the great plateau of Slamannan and Shotts and, if the weather was very good, the sharp pimple of Tinto Hill, down by Biggar, punctuated the horizon. To the east, rose the Pentlands. West were the Campsie Fells and Touch Hills. But these were distant places yet to be explored. For now, I was 'king' of the Tullibody Woods.

The Tullibody Woods have a long history. They appear as two massive square blocks of forest in Roy's map of 1749, stretching on either side of the Tullibody-Alloa road towards the River Devon in the north and the policies of Tullibody House in the south. The First Statistical Account of the 1790s describes that "between 60 and 70 years ago" (c1720-1730) a large (140 acre) rugged piece of ground to the east of the village was enclosed and planted with firs. When they were 40 to 50 years old (c1760-1780) they were cut and sold and the ground planted with oaks.

Over the years since the First Statistical Account, the woods would have been felled and replanted many times with different species and mixes of trees. In the same time, the shape of the woods has changed. Parts have been felled and converted to farmland. The First Statistical Account tells us that Mr Erskine, about 14 years previous, had built a farmhouse and created a farm out of "a dreary and uncultivated waste" and created enclosures, clumps, belts and strips of planting on what would become Lornshill. The map of 1899 shows the shape of Tullibody Woods in 1899. The farms of Muirside, Muirpark, King o' Muirs and Lornshill have all brought parts of the woodland into cultivation and the remaining woods are sub-divided into North Wood, Blackmuir Wood and Delph Wood.

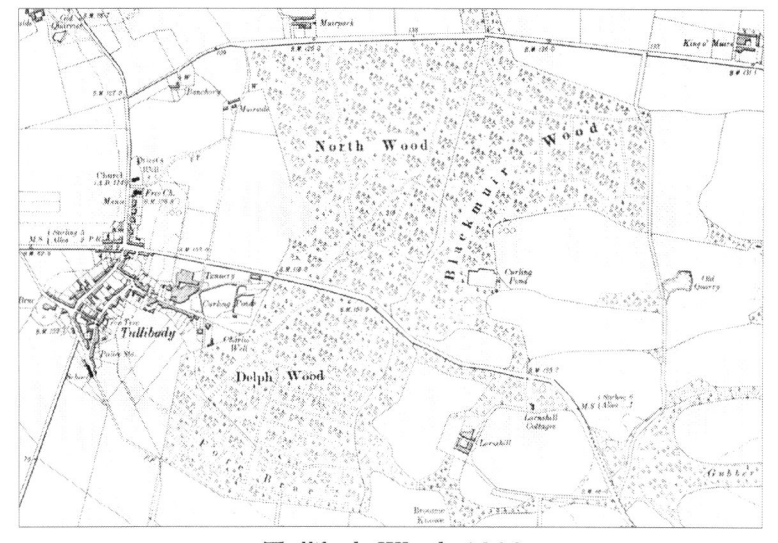

Tullibody Woods 1899
'Reproduced with the permission of the National Library of Scotland'

These were the woods as I knew them, more or less, in the 1940s and 50s. The borders and layout of the rides in the Delph Wood fits with the pine plantation I grew up in, although part of the area identified as Fore Brae, above the present golf course, was an open area of bracken and the section just east of the Delph Pond was under scrub birch. The largely deciduous oaks and beeches of Blackmuir Wood is where Geordie, the gamekeeper, took me trapping, save that a significant area north of the curling pond had already been cleared and formed a small heather moorland. Likewise, North Wood on the map was no longer a wood, but an area of heather, birch and gorse known locally as the 'Ham and Egg Braes', reputedly from a recent history of pig and chicken production!

For much of my boyhood these woods were my garden, my Empire, my world. When I was deemed to be old enough to venture out of sight of the house at Woodside Terrace - the woods were my home. It took many years to achieve my treetop eyrie. Many years of apprenticeship - of learning the secret paths through the pine trees, where we tracked as Indian hunters or loped as 'runners of the wood' in the best Hollywood tradition. I was not always alone. We were not so much a 'gang' - more a loose confederation of individuals, a network of like-minded souls garnered from school, Cubs, Scouts and neighbours who flowed in and out of the group as and when the particular ploy appealed to them - or whatever their boredom threshold was on the day. Names come and go in the memory, but at one time or another, names to remember include - Scott Cameron, David Young, Alex McGregor, Jim McManus, "Nipper" McCann. All went off to build their own careers in life - but may recall from time to time their adventures in the Tullibody Woods.

On any one day we were Red Indians stalking through the undergrowth following unsuspecting pensioners out for their daily constitutional. More energetically, we were Indian hunters, chasing reluctant pigeons, pheasants and rabbits with primitive bows and arrows. We morphed into big-game hunters digging elephant-pits on known elephant trails, cunningly camouflaged with freshly-cut bracken. No elephants are recorded and no unsuspecting pensioners either - a blessing. Every Indian or hunter needs an encampment and huts were a perpetual source of fun and drama. Fallen trees created lean-to shelters. Forestry drains could be roofed over and disguised with pine needles. We had huts and shelters all over the woods with different levels of design and sophistication. They had to be 'SECRET'. Once rumbled, they were targeted by other gangs and knocked down. Great efforts were made to build them in inaccessible places - hence my eventual and final success - my eyrie at the top of my Scots Pine survived the longest.

At the same time as we were hunting elephants and endangering pensioners, we absorbed the nature and ways of the wildlife of the woods. The places where the foxes hid, the pigeons nested and the sparrow hawks hunted. Sitting quietly under the canopy and letting the birds tell us everything that was happening throughout the wood. Learning the language of the birds, the songs marking their territories, where we could look for nests. Their alarm calls, warning us that something was not right in their corner of the woods. By osmosis, we picked up knowledge of the other wildlife - insects like the frightening wood wasp with its long spike; the difference between voles and shrews, willow-herb and ragged robin, mushrooms and poisonous fungi. Wonders no classroom could teach.

And then, one day a strange caravan appeared among the birch trees. A genuine gypsy caravan, two Clydesdale horses, a long four-wheeled trailer and a family of travellers - including Ken. Ken was my age - plus or minus. He was small, wiry and the colour of a ripe chestnut. He had spent his young life living in woods across the country. We got on fine. Ken came to school, as he did wherever his family's work took them. His folk were woodcutters and about to make a dramatic change to the Tullibody Woods. They set up camp in what was then a birch wood to the east of the Delph Pond, where is now Westview Crescent. Over a period, with manual tools and horse-power, they cleared the birch scrub and logged the first substantial part of Delph Wood.

At the time it was all so exciting. Playing with Ken produced lots of adventures. As the clearance got under way huge piles of tree roots and brushings created vast networks of tunnels through which we crawled, like shrews, for hours on end. The results of any collapse would be unthinkable. But then….? - no Health and Safety in those days. We got to walk with real horses, great gentle brutes with huge hooves and hairy legs, clanking chains and creaking leather. We got to ride on the waggon. Eventually we got to ride on the horses after the day's work when they were led to the Delph for the evening drink and wash. Here came the disaster, well, embarrassment really. It was fine sitting bareback on the horse on the level ground. To get to the Delph to drink it had to descend a steepish banking. The horse tilted forward down the slope, then lowered its neck to drink and I slid forward down its back, over its neck into the water. So much for a cowboy!

I did not grudge the clearance at the time. In some ways it was inevitable. Tullibody was expanding. New houses were needed but looking back at it now, we did not appreciate the extent of the transformation to come. Ken did manage to preserve my special rowan tree until near the end of the clearance. This was an ancient specimen whose gnarled branches twisted in just the right way to create three comfortable armchairs some twenty feet above the ground. It was difficult to climb into unless you were us. We knew the way to reach, stretch and swing just so - to swing up into the branches and our leafy armchairs above the lesser mortals below. But, with the partial clearance of the Delph Wood, our world had been violated. Secret parts of our forest were no longer secret. Tracks and paths opened up access for others. 'Pitch and Toss' games appeared in secluded areas. It was time to move on.

The Fields

From the lounge window of Woodside Terrace, across the Alloa Road, the fields of Muirside Farm stretched. Throughout each summer we watched them change from green to yellow to gold, as the crop ripened - oats, wheat or barley. Then one day the tractor would arrive - a little Fergie, a Davie Brown or a bigger Massey-Ferguson - heralded by much noise and towing a binder.

The Fields - from Woodside lounge window

This was the signal we small boys had been waiting for. As soon as the first strip had been cut around the field, the game was on. Over the spring and summer a large portion of the rabbit population of the Braes had adopted the field for food and shelter. As the cutting progressed and the square of remaining crop shrank the rabbits were concentrated in the middle - until they panicked. This was our reversion to Stone Age hunters. Armed with sticks, stones and garden tools we waited for the rabbits to bolt from cover and then chased them enthusiastically. I don't recall catching many but the thrill of the chase was exciting. The professionals did it better. John Shaw - Mr Shaw to us - was the gamekeeper on the Braes and on this field and knew how to pot rabbits. He stood well back, away from the cutting and the small boys, waited until the rabbits were almost clear of the field and got them with his twelve-bore shotgun. At the end of the day we might have a rabbit for the larder.

Further away, were Andrew Hendry's fields. Andrew was in our class at Primary School. A great lad with three big strapping elder brothers who worked Northfield Farm, out west, near Manor Powis. Edgar and I cycled there frequently and had the freedom of Andrew's fields, farmyard and orchard. A small stream ran through the land and provided endless days of fun. The orchard supplied too many green apples with predictable results. In later years when we had to earn money, the neighbouring farm of Midtown, at Blackgrange, always needed workers for the hay. We built young muscles as well as hay-ricks out in the hot and thirsty fields. The farmer was always at pains to show us the newspaper cutting purporting the show that we were getting the correct rate of pay for our age and status. We were never sure of the date or year of the cutting which seems to appear the same each summer! Out in the thirsty fields we drank a powerful potion of water laced with oatmeal, kept cool in the shade of a hay-rick. It still sounds unpleasant but it was nectar out there on a hot day. We ate our own breakfast and lunch in the farm bothy, half a dozen of us. Not quite 'bothy ballads' but great fun and Mum's cheese and lettuce sandwiches washed down with a flask of strong tea never tasted so good. Eventually, summer jobs took me out of the fields and on to Cambus Distillery, where the barley from the fields was transformed into something entirely different. The money was better - but I missed my summers in the fields.

Tullibody School

"I go out through the gap in the hedge, turn right along the bank of the Delph, down Delph Road, left into Manor Crescent, right up the hidden lane to Main Street, along past the Tron Tree, Duncan's chickens, McKechnie's sweetie shop, across Park Terrace and I am in Tullibody School playground."

On my transfer from my Glasgow school I recall I was put into a class below my Glasgow school. It must have been deemed that Glasgow boys were less intelligent than those of Tullibody. My first teacher was a Miss Ewan. Miss Ewan had been a teacher at Tullibody when my mother had been at school but made no connection between the Jamieson name and the Dallas one. Ms Ewan seemed to think that, as a Glasgow boy, I needed extra discipline as the 'beltings', for no apparent reason, became rather frequent. This continued until my mother made an appearance, in front of her former, and now much older teacher, to enquire the reason - and the victimisation was transferred to some other unfortunate pupils.

Main Street. c. 1950s

This was a time when Tullibody was just beginning to expand in response to an expected increase in coal-mining. Miners were coming through from the west to develop the Manor and the new Glenochil collieries. The long-established village names - Blair, Fotheringham, Starkie, McKinven - were being joined by new names - Mushet, Fullarton, Leckie, Penman - some bringing a different culture and behaviour to a still-rural community. Inevitably this brought conflict to the playground as new pecking-orders were established. Nevertheless, I made many friends among the 'incomers' at school and many more in the Cubs and Scout troops.

THE BRAE AT THE BAINGLE

BAINGLE BRAE

Having squeezed into Gran's house at Woodside Terrace for more than a year, we moved to 28 Baingle Brae in 1950. This was at the west end of the village, open to the fields across the road. There was a fine view of Dumyat and the Ochil Hills to the north and an unlimited vista to the west as far as Ben Lomond, Ben Ledi and the other big mountains of the Southern Highlands.

I moved to the new Abercromby School in 1951 for my last two Primary years under Mr Easton.

Abercromby School, Primary 6. c 1951

Coincidental with my knowledge of birds, I had developed some talent in bird-impersonation. This quirk was picked up by another teacher, Mrs McKendrick, who ran a choir called 'The Abercromby Junior Singers'. I was given a slot on their programme, to do 'Bird Impressions' and participated in most of the choir engagements around the local area. This led to an audition for the BBC Children's Hour in 1954.

Abercromby School, Primary 7. c1952.

Abercromby Junior Singers. c. 1950

Scouting

I had joined the Cubs when I was old enough and enjoyed our evenings with Akela, Baloo and Baghera, followed by a poke of chips from the 'chippie' on the way home. We met in the ex-army wooden hut in Stirling Road just west of the Cross. I made many friends in the Cubs and was ready to move up to the Scouts in due course.

Tullibody Cubs man a Coronation float. 1953.

Jock Dewar was our Scoutmaster - our 'Skip' - and also the District Commissioner. He was supported by a fine group of Scouters seen in the photograph. John Pryde I remember because he became the Scoutmaster later when I was a Scouter.

The outdoor activities appealed to me. Weekend camps at Blairingone started with the May Holiday and were rarely missed. Cooking porridge and soot over a wood fire was only matched by potato hash and charcoal for dinner. Rabbits were chased, trees were climbed, rivers were swum. Our favourite game was 'puddicks'- a cross between baseball, rounders and cricket using a rough piece of wood sourced from the forest.

My first Summer Camp took me to Scone Palace grounds in an open truck, where we swam in a backwater of the River Tay, and stepped on flounders and eels.

Tullibody Scouts, Jock Dewar and Scouters c. 1955
Can you find: John Pryde, Alex Main, Leonard Silverstone, Nick Penman, Tam Gould, 'Nipper' McCann, Stewart Bryce, David Young, Bert Scott, Ian Brady, Alex Scott?

The Scouts introduced me to serious hiking. The first proper hike I recall was a solo tramp from Baingle Brae, Tullibody to Menstrie, then along the A91 to Blairlogie, Logie Kirk and Causewayhead to get the bus home. It was short hike but the first by my 14-year old self and I proudly wrote it up methodically in the approved style. Another hike was from the bus stop at Helensfield, Clackmannan, to Dollar via Forestmill, Aberdona and Dollarbeg. As a real 'tramp' I had my tin 'billy' and made tea over a wood fire somewhere outside Forestmill. It was a great adventure.

Hiking was an integral part of the Boy Scout experience. There were patrol hikes and walks from camps. My school-friend, Alex Scott, from Tillicoultry, buddied me on my First Class Journey - an overnight 14-mile hike around Sheriffmuir - and I went with him on his First Class Journey by Crook of Devon to Solsgirth and the Cleish Hills, camping at Crook of Devon.

At one time I had the privilege to lead the Curlew Patrol, with Donald MacAngus as Second, and in due course gained, what I believe, was Tullibody Scouts first Queen's Scout award. I represented Clackmannanshire at the 1957 Jamboree in Sutton Coldfield and went on to become a Rover Scout and Scouter under John Pryde, helping to run a Summer Camp near Balquhidder in 1959.

On Patrol - Summer Camp Balquhidder. 1959

At that time we had a powerful group of young Scouts growing in confidence and ability. Three of them were christened - the 'Three Musketeers' - Robert Anderson, John Frew and Duncan Bremner - each of whom went on to become Queen's Scouts, in their own turn, and to serve the Scout movement in Clackmannanshire as Scouters and Commissioners. Robert Anderson led the patrol which won the County Flag in 1960.

Tullibody Scouts, 1960

County Flag Patrol, 1960

Robert Anderson receiving the County Flag from Major Tullis, 1960

The Reward. Robert Anderson with County Flag

The River Forth

"Then I hear what I have come to hear - the low cackling of geese, pink-footed geese. The voices grow louder, borne down the wind to me. Above the trees to the west. In the grey dawn I can just make out a fine, waving line of them above the sea wall. Two shots ring out but none of the geese falter. They come downwind, a great skein of about 100 birds, now stretching out across the sky, now telescoping into a close-knit pack of wings and bodies. The eastern sky grows lighter as they disappear behind the trees of Throsk."

The River Forth at Cambus

As soon as I was old enough, Uncle Willie walked me down to the tidal part of the River Devon at Cambus, ostensibly to catch flounders. The Devon was not then the relatively clean river it is now. A whisky distillery had been founded in Cambus since 1806 and taken over by the Distillers Company in 1877. The Forth River Purification Board was not established until 1950s and by the time the Devon reached Cambus it carried much of the effluent of two distilleries, several mines and the sewage and industrial effluent of the Hillfoots towns - out to the North Sea via the Forth. The water and mud had a particular odour which could only be ignored by dedicated fishermen. The flounders were obviously not impressed and I doubt whether we would have been able to eat them anyway but only the odd eel came to our baits wriggling and twisting up the line, creating terrible tangles and very slippery. But the magic spell was cast.

The weir at Cambus

The River Forth was more accessible from Baingle Brae. The river is tidal and the tide creeps up the Devon as far as the weir at Cambus - but no further. Depending on the time, the tide in the Forth can be quite strong and twice a day the ebb and flood sweeps in food. It is a rich feeding place for water birds and their predators. It was favourite spot for bird watching and, for a fan of Peter Scott, the 'dawn flight' was always a must-see.

December 27 1957.

"It was dark when I arrived at the seawall, very dark. It was an hour before dawn when I dumped my bike and followed the vague line of the path to the water. A fair easterly breeze was blowing. Goldeneye rose up on whistling wings. Mallard and teal were noisy somewhere out in the darkness. I sat on a log and waited. The gulls began to come over - long, ghostly trains, floating over the river, lifting over the dyke and slipping down low again to avoid the wind, silent. Then the curlews started. Just an occasional 'pipe' at first. The a pack of them came twisting down the river in full-blooded cry. Soon it was light enough to see the ducks out on the water. Then the geese came."

Summer was also good for birds on the Forth. In July the reed beds would be full of 'churring' sedge warblers. Wader families were everywhere - lapwing, curlew, snipe, redshank, oyster-catcher. Shelduck families paddled on the mud around Tullibody Inch. A spoonbill was reported between Kincardine and the Black Devon but we never did find it.

> *"…..These were the woods the river and sea*
> *Where a boy*
> *In the listening*
> *Summertime of the dead whispered the truth of his joy*
> *To the trees and the stones and the fish in the tide.*
> *And the mystery*
> *Sang alive*
> *Still in the water and singingbirds. "*

From "Poem in October" by Dylan Thomas

FURTHER HORIZONS

FURTHER HORIZONS

I went up to senior secondary school - Alloa Academy - at the end of summer 1953. I thoroughly enjoyed my time there, finding new horizons in academic, social and sporting directions. Academically, I enjoyed the new subjects - with varying degrees of proficiency. Maths was not a strong point. I have trouble visualising my world in numbers - even arithmetic. I got through by learning by rote and, surprisingly, passed Higher Maths. History and German were options I missed out on. Science - Physics and Chemistry - were interesting but not interesting enough. I enjoyed learning French as a new language. I must have enjoyed English. I can still recall snippets of Shakespeare and distant Sonnets by rote but I think the course unconsciously opened up my imagination to the power of words and sounds, which I still enjoy today. My prime academic interest however was Geography. Most aspects of Geography produced some enthusiasm - the natural aspects of geology, landscape and ecology, through the varieties of foreign countries to the spatial aspects of surveying and recording in the field.

I had decided when I went to senior school, that I needed to be more assertive than I had been at primary school. In the end this was not really necessary. At the Academy I found many more kindred spirits, who shared my interests and attitudes and I fitted in just fine. I chummed- up with Alex Scott from Tillicoultry. I am not sure now how we got together but we were both Scouts and keen on the outdoors - bird watching and fishing. My main outlet for any assertiveness I found on the rugby pitch. My main contribution to school-life was through the Film Society. This had been set up two years previously by two students - Bobby Dickson and Roy Court - who were in my sister Ann's year. Both gentlemen went on to do great things in cinema - Bobby Dickson ending up in Hollywood as a producer. In 1954 they needed a projectionist and perhaps Ann volunteered her brother - I never did find out how I got the job. When Bobby and Roy left school I was left running the show with my friend - Edgar Cherry - as fellow projectionist and it was a great entree into school social life.

Alloa Academy Prefects, 1959

Rugby was my sport at school. I enjoyed rugby from the start and my stature and terrier-like attitude marked me out for a scrum-half - a position I played in every rugby game I entered - even into the RAF. We played widely across Central Scotland - Queen Victoria School, Dunblane; Grangemouth High; Stirling High; Dollar Academy; Dunfermline High and Queen Margaret's; Bell-Baxter, Cupar; Buckhaven and Kirkcaldy. I played for the Firsts in 1958 and earned my 'colours' in 1959. I must have been fit in those days. I would play rugby for school in the morning and play football for the Scouts in the afternoon, cycle everywhere and still be out in the evening. Ah!

Those never-to-be-forgotten days! We moved up to the new Academy in 1958 and I graduated with enough Highers to go to University.

Alloa Academy Rugby First XV, 1959

During these years, Dad was at sea until 1954 when he was hospitalised with TB. He went into Alloa ID Hospital in 1955, more or less for the rest of my school days. I used to organise evening film shows for him and his fellow-patients and Edgar Cherry and I took turns as projectionists. Dad died in 1974 and was cremated in Falkirk.

Mum, at various times, worked part-time in Mrs Fraser's shop at the Cross and weighed the babies as a volunteer at the baby clinic. She was active in the church as founder-Secretary, and then President, of the Women's Guild and eventually one of the first lady elders in the Church of Scotland. Mum died in 2000 and her ashes are scattered at Blairlogie.

Sister Ann had joined the Sauchie Girl Guides and remained in the Guide movement for the rest of her life. She represented the Guides at the 1953 Coronation and went on to become a

Queen's Guide, a Guide Captain and District Commissioner. Our family visits to the Sauchie Guide summer camps at Strathyre were always memorable. Ann met her future husband David Mudie at Alloa Academy. They were married in 1962 and started married life in Tullibody, before moving to 'Hillside' in Alloa. Peter Mudie was born in 1967, followed by Andrew, in 1969 and David, in 1972. The family moved to Norwood Avenue, Alloa, where Ann stayed until her death in 2013. Ann's ashes are interred in the kirkyard at Eassie, Angus.

The Ochil Hills

The Ochil Hills

"The short grass vibrates with small black butterflies. It is July. Somewhere up ahead Grandad is telling me it isn't far to go. For a five-year old it is a steep hill. Up from Menstrie village, climbing the track up the east side of Dumyat, heading for a picnic in Menstrie Glen with Gran, Grandad, Mum and sister Ann. Above the trees I can look back over the roofs of Menstrie, the first time I have been able to look down on roofs, rather than up at them. The magic of height. It is hot and I am weary. "Not far now", says Grandad. Up ahead the path eases and forks right, following a narrow sheep-track downhill. The shady trees and cool waters of Menstrie Glen lie below."

This was my introduction to walking in the Ochil Hills. As with so much of early life, it was Grandad who led the way. Menstrie

Glen was his favourite and I first set foot on the Ochils on one of his picnic expeditions to Menstrie Glen. From Ochil Street there were tantalising glimpses of Dumyat and Ben Cleuch, between other houses. From Woodside Terrace, the front window was filled by Craigleith and Myreton Hill and, on many of our walks, with Grandad, around Tullibody, the whole impressive south-facing scarp of the Ochils could be seen. They were the background of our lives and important weather checks. *"If you can't see Dumyat - it is raining. If you can see it - it is about to rain"* - ran the local saying, not without foundation. So it was a natural progression for a young boy growing up in Tullibody to want to go to the hills. An appreciation of the nature of the Ochil Hills stemmed from these early walks with Grandad:

> *"Frequent rests and sitting down shows that the tiny black butterflies are, in fact, deep blue, with spots underneath. Other butterflies dance in the heat, brown with mottled patches and spots. The tiny yellow flowers around my feet have four petals, set in a star. Blue bell-like flowers line the path. Other yellow flowers have lots of little petals up and down the stem. Grasshoppers grate in the distance and suddenly erupt from the grass when you go to pick them up."*

Later, many of my travels in the Ochils were motivated by fishing or climbing but there were endless days of gentle exploration of the secret parts of the Menstrie Glen, Dumyat and Sheriffmuir. The birdlife was everywhere. Wheatears were the harbinger of spring and followed us up the hillsides. Curlews were the sound of spring, their cries rippling across the glen. Sheriffmuir had a good red grouse population.

27 June 1956. Cocksburn Reservoir had a pair of great crested grebes nesting, together with a pair of swans with 3 cygnets, redshank, sandpiper, moorhen, reed bunting and 6 coot.

19 July 1956. A trip to Dumyat and Menstrie recorded kestrel, wheatear, meadow pipit, skylark, chaffinch, redstart,

whinchat, willow warblers, cuckoo, mistle thrush, wood pigeons, curlew, and lapwing. Other trips record ravens near the high tops and there was usually a peregrine on Dumyat and, very occasionally, a buzzard and merlin.

Alex Scott's father was a shepherd on the Ochils and Alex knew the hills well. We hiked the Ochils - Wood Hill, Elistoun, The Law, Ben Cleuch, Andrew Gannel Hill, Maddy Moss, Skythorn and King's Seat. We hiked the glens when fishing the burns - Daiglen, Gannel, Brioch, Grodwell, Frandy, Sherup and Devon. We cycled and camped at Blairingone, Dunning Glen, Upper Frandy Reservoir. We were camping, with Edgar Cherry, in the snow at Loch Lubnaig, Strathyre, went Alex's health problem became apparent and we had to be evacuated home by Edgar's Dad. Alex wasn't able to do much tramping after that. I continued to explore the western Ochils - Dumyat, Coalsnaur, Blairdenon and Loss Hill and fished Balquharn, Menstrie and Wharry burns for trout.

Climbing

My serious interest in mountaineering was sparked by my school visit to Glenmore Lodge Outdoor Centre in the Cairngorms in June 1957. Here we got the training and the challenges and I loved it. We scoured the Rothiemurchus Forest and the Cairngorms. I still have the map with all the routes marked on it. Clach Barraig bothy, Chalamain Gap. Our big adventure was climbing up and over Cairngorm (in 82 degrees C!) over to Coire Raibert, Loch Avon, the Shelter Stone and up to Loch Etchachan for the bivouac. I recall a very young RAF Canberra navigator, with us as a volunteer guide, playing the chanter as we sat having lunch in the sun in Coire Raibert. His name was Flight Lieutenant Alec Wedderburn. I was to bump into Alec several time in my later RAF career. Next day was Ben Macdhui, Coire Sneachda, Coire Lochain, Jean's Hut and back to base. Magic. One of the fellow students at Glenmore was a quiet but very keen chap called Russell Sharp also from Tillicoultry. After Glenmore we did a few walks in the Ochils together including a New Year's Day climb to King's Seat, Andrew Gannel Hill, Ben Cleuch and The Law - in wonderful snow conditions with crampons and ice axes. Russell went into the laboratory at Cambus Distillery and in later life he bought and operated Caledonian Brewery in Edinburgh. He continued his mountaineering career with some big stuff in the Himalayas.

On another memorable winter day I took a party of younger Scouts up from Menstrie to Blairdenon to pay our respects at the site of a recently crashed Tiger Moth aircraft which had claimed the life of a young Air Training Corps pilot. A young Geoffrey Inglis was on that trek - who went on to a career in serious mountaineering.

Dumyat provided many adventures. One winter day, with Andrew Black, a Scottish Schools sprint champion, we set off from Menstrie in thick fog. Just below the summit we came out on top of the fog to a clear blue sky and unlimited visibility above a sea of cloud. With no camera we scree-ran down the face of Dumyat, collected Andrew's camera and ran back up again to take our pictures. We were fit in those days!

King's Seat Hill - January 1959

The rock on much of the Ochils was too crumbly for serious rock climbing. The gully in the centre of the Craigleith cliff was wet and mossy and caused a retreat. There is a firm little crag at the back of Dumyat useful for practice but much of the face of Dumyat is very friable. The best 'named' route is Raeburn's Gully in the eastern side of the central cleft of Dumyat. This was a one-off solo climb for me and proved to be a challenge - easier to go up than get down again. But I survived.

Worth the double climb - Craigleith above the fog from Dumyat

Trout Fishing

Alex Scott and I were also fishing buddies. Our first casts with a fly rod were on the River Devon one summers' evening we made our way down to where the road, railway and river all come together on the corner just outside Tillicoultry on the road to Dollar. There, we waded across the river and thrashed the water for a few idyllic hours, more in hope than expectation. The seed was sown but we would concentrate on worm-fishing for the next few years.

Alex's Dad, Ian, was shepherd on that whole swathe of hill east of Tillicoultry Burn, up on to the Cleuch and out as far as Maddy Moss. There was no part of that hill that he didn't know and he passed the knowledge on the Alex and myself. With growing confidence we explored further. Alex and I had fished the Gannel Burn, above Tillicoultry on many days before either of us caught our first trout. Setting off in the early morning with very basic kit - Alex's recycled aerial from a WW2 tank and my remaining six feet of an old 9-foot greenheart rod - we would fish the accessible pools on the Tillicoultry Burn and then turn right, up the Gannel, leap-frogging each other from pool to pool, trying to be polite about sharing the most likely bits but secretly competing to catch the most – or any - trout.

Alex on the Gannel

It was a long, but great, apprenticeship of exhilarating days in the rain or the sun, when the excuses for failure were many – too cold, too bright, water too low! Eventually we gained the knowledge - which pools held the biggest trout; dull weather was best; a little colour in the water was helpful; when the trout fed – and empty baskets became less frequent. The Daiglen had good fishing pools. The Burn of Sorrow could be reached over the watershed from the Gannel. One memorable day we crossed the watershed at Maddy Moss and like 'stout Cortez' viewing the Pacific – we looked down the valley of the Brioch, to the great lowland of Strathearn and the vast rampart of the Grampian Mountains beyond. Our horizons had suddenly exploded. Down the Brioch we fished and up the Grodwell. One long summer's day of east wind and clear blue sky we got, not exactly lost, but 'temporarily unsure of our position!' We had fished up the Gannel and down the Brioch, crossed the ridge to fish down the Frandy and then set off for home - only to find ourselves in Glen Sherup. It was a long hungry hike back to Tillicoultry, but Leah Scott's banana sponge and fresh scones refuelled me for my cycle back to Tullibody.

Three or four of us - Alex, David, Murray, Edgar - were all keen fishers at that time and Menstrie was an early focus. From early casts in the pools of the main Menstrie burn, we explored the three Inchna tributaries. David's fishing diaries record days of 30 to 50 small trout, all put back in the water. An eight-inch trout was a good one, a ten-inch fish was a monster with associated 'bragging-rights'. The search for bigger fish soon took us to the reservoirs. March 15 is the opening of the brown trout season and saw us for several years of our youth sitting frozen among the trees at Wharry Dam (Waltersmuir Reservoir) watching the sleet drift past and expecting our worms to catch the occasional, thin early-season trout. The important thing was to be out at the start of the season after the barren months of winter. Lossburn Reservoir and Balquharn Dam were other early-season expeditions with the occasional cast on Cocksburn, which was strictly preserved.

A life-changing trip for me was a solo expedition from Balquharn Dam, up to the big pool below the waterfall, the Grey Mare's Tail, then further up the burn, deep into the glen. Lack of success tempted me up the hillside onto the ridge between Coalsnaur and Bengengie and then into the morass of Menstrie Moss. Eventually negotiating the peat-hags and the green quaking mosses I reached the Wharry Burn under the blue shoulder of Blairdenon and fished it down to the Sheriffmuir Road. It was a long walk home to Menstrie and cycle back to Tullibody.

Eventually we graduated to fly-fishing and spread our wings beyond the Ochils. The River Devon was our next adventure. At Easter 1955 we strapped camping gear onto our bikes and set up base in Dunning Glen by the Glendey burn. Further up the Dunning road we found ourselves in the headwaters of the South Queich, catching pure-silver fingerlings, like small salmon, the progeny of the big trout which migrated upstream from Loch Leven to spawn in the back-end. Alex died, all too young, in 1967 - 26 years old - and business took me far away.

The Fishing

The burn flowed down the hillside
Like a tousled collie. We climbed and climbed.
A spit of rain in the air; edges of sky
Furred with mist. And there, the loch, at last,
Like a gem in the brooch of the moors.

The canvas bag with the rod,
The sizzle of the reel,
The search for the best place to cast.

I chased a blue gust of damselflies
Then sat and listened to the silence;
The huge emptiness of the hills
Buried under a rubble of cloud.

There was always one fish, slippery
And the heathery smoke of a fire,
Till the dark sank and the rain began for good.

I see it now, years back across the moorland,
That what mattered was not the fish at all
But everything else.

Kenneth C Steven

The Island of Iona

Ian Cowie points the way. Iona

I first experienced the magic of Iona in the 1950s, helping with a group of young people from St Serf's Church Youth Club. Ian Cowie was the minister and an inspirational leader. On Iona, George MacLeod was still very much in evidence. The Abbey roof was complete but the site still rang to the hammers of the stone masons. We lived in wooden huts and explored an almost deserted island, packed with little hills, hidden valleys, bays, beaches, caves and other secret corners all with musical Gaelic names which translate into places like *"The Bay at the Back of the Ocean"*, *"The Cairn of the Back to Ireland"* or *"The Well at the Dell of the Cock"*.

Our pilgrimage to Iona was quite as exciting as the rest of our stay there. There were no car ferries in those days. The ancient ferry - the "Lochinvar"- took us from Oban, across the mouth of Loch Linnhe towards Mull, while its passengers huddled down below to escape the sudden squalls and flying spray. The ferry did not dock at Craignure either. Instead we were transferred gingerly aboard a launch, rising and falling, badly out of unison with the larger vessel. This accomplished, we put about for the jetty, while the "Lochinvar" buffeted its way on to Tobermory.

The journey across Mull was in a ten-seat minibus into which were crushed fourteen bodies plus a few suitcases, all eyes straining for the sight of red deer in Glen More and otters along Loch Scridain. At Fionnphort, a motor launch ferried us in a wide sweep across the Sound - to Iona. Soon we were tucking into a welcome tea and settled into our wooden dormitory huts amid the sound of the seemingly constant wind.

One or two images remain in the mind. Ceilidhs, with other visitors, in the Abbey refectory were packed with hilarious entertainment. Then there were 'spooky' stories, told with feeling by 'Our Leader - the Reverend Ian Cowie. These covered many of the legends of Iona and the Hebrides, while we listened enthralled in a candlelit nook in the Library.

One unforgettable character on Iona at that time was - Willie. Irish by birth, a rover by nature, he sported a virile beard from ear-to-ear, hair that not seen clippers for months and a grin that thawed any atmosphere. Disdaining shoes all year round, he performed his daily duties of stoking, painting and helping around the Abbey, in his bare feet, a pair of ragged trousers, a sweater and fur-lined waistcoat. A rugged piratical appearance with a heart of gold, Willie had seen a fair bit of life in his 20-odd years. Ex-public school in Belfast, he had drifted around, working wherever he could, serving on mine-sweepers and hitch-hiking around the country.

Willie introduced us to Easter swimming among the seals of Port Ban. At a barefoot trot, he led us over the bog and rock of the North End to that sandy cove on the west side of the island. There, in the clear water, played half a dozen grey seals, eyeing us inquisitively with their heads bobbing on the surface or drawn up lethargically sunbathing on Harp Rock in the centre of the bay. A quick in-and-out dip was all that we visitors could survive but Willie be-sported himself like Old Neptune.

Further horizons over a sunlit sea

Other explorations of the island took us to Spouting Cave, where long Atlantic rollers thunder into a narrow crack and shoot a sixty-foot plume of spray into the air. A visit to the Marble Quarry introduced us to the unique marble, a beautiful green and white form, best-seen in the communion table of the Abbey itself. No trip to the island would be complete without an ascent of its highest hill - Dun-I, a full 322 feet above the sea.

The Abbey was particularly impressive during evening service when candles cast a warm glow over the pews, the piano echoed in the darkened vaults of the roof while the wind sighed or shrieked around the solid square tower of the Abbey. It was a wonderful sanctuary of peace and beauty. Little worries disappeared, outlooks widened and presented a different perspective on life and fellowship. Iona was a composition of colours - rock, sea and sky, intense or subtle or sun or moon; sounds and smells of surf, seabirds and wind; memories of varied characters and interests, who forgot their shyness, class and affectations to be friends.

Returning to Iona in 2004, I came across a powerful poem - *"Atlantic"* - by a young poet, Kenneth C Steven. We became friends.

'Atlantic'

Every January I hear the Atlantic
It blows in with the wind at night, a high tide
To swell around my bed, to salt my mouth,
And whisper out before the morning.

And afterwards, for days, all other time is washed away,
Except the time of that rolling ocean.
It becomes my blood, becomes the salty flow
That beats the drum of my life.

Until I go, until I leave and go out west
Stand and listen to all that has been calling me,
Try to translate what I was hearing
Another spring, another year, without succeeding.

Kenneth C Steven

Contrails

"It is a cold frosty morning in the Ochils. The sky is cloudless, a clear blue with unlimited visibility. Soon, strange etchings appear high up in the eastern sky - narrow, white trails of cloud-like vapour tracing patterns across the blue. Two sets of circles form, joined by two more, curving, curling and twisting across the sky. The fighter squadrons from RAF Leuchars are airborne and practicing their interceptions. I want to be up there with them."

My passion for aircraft and flying goes back a long way. It is 1946. I sit on a dyke in a grimy, claustrophobic back-court, off the Maryhill Road, in Glasgow, and watch, in wonder, as a thin, white line creeps across the postage-stamp of pale blue sky, which is all that is visible above the towering walls of the enclosing tenements. The white line appears above the roofs of Wilton Street, draws a straight line due south and disappears above the roofs of Raeberry Street. It thickens and spreads into an ethereal, wispy cloud as it grows. At its head, a small silver cross identifies the source of this wonder - an aeroplane, flying very high, leaving a trail of condensed vapour. I have no real idea what type of aeroplane it is but what it stands for, crossing that small restricted piece of sky, is freedom - a freedom to move across horizons, unconstrained by tenements, roads and the grubbieness of post-war Glasgow.

Some time, before Dad went back to sea, he took me down to the Clyde Model Dockyard in the Argyle Arcade. We bought a rubber-powered model aeroplane, built by Frog, with detachable wings and a tubular aluminium fuselage. We took it for its test flight. We placed it in a cradle in its box, wound up the rubber band and launched it skywards. Of course, it crashed, many times, but it was a robust little machine and, despite the setbacks, it flew - and the magic of flight was born. Kits of solid balsa wood followed - Supermarine Attacker, Grumman Panther, Hawker Hunter. Keil Kraft sold rubber-powered flying kits made from a balsa wood framework covered in paper, tautened with aircraft dope. Dad helped me build the first one - an Auster Autocrat, high-wing monoplane. It flew well until someone stood on it. Next came a bright blue Stinson, then an orange Beechcraft Bonanza, a Luscombe Silvaire, a Grumman Cougar and then a light-blue De Haviland Chipmunk, which flew like a dream and lasted a long time. After the flying models came the Airfix plastic kits with my Lancaster and Spitfire having pride of place.

Hollywood of course had its part to play. *High Flight* and *The Dam Busters* were in the cinemas. The *Eagle* comic had wonderful cut-away drawings of all the latest British aircraft. 'Battle of Britain' days at RAF Turnhouse fired the imagination and set me on course for a flying career.

The Future: A Canberra bomber at RAF Turnhouse, 1956

I set off for Glasgow in October 1959 - my "Time Called Tullibody" - had run out.

AUTHOR

Drew Jamieson trained as a geographer. His first career spanned 20 years as a pilot and flying instructor in the Royal Air Force. His further career included fisheries management, conservation and environmental planning in local government and the water industry. His writings have been published in The Scotsman, The Scottish Field, The Atlantic Salmon Journal and other angling magazines.

email: dumyat2@btinternet.com

"The fairy time o life, Tam,
Its noo the time of yore!
And whatna lovely world we lost
When boyhood's hour was o'er."

Remembering Alex Scott
1941-1967.

FURTHER ENJOYMENT

Corbett, Roy and Snaddon. *The Ochil Hills: An Introduction: Landscape, Wildlife, Heritage, Walks.* Forth Naturalist and Historian/Clackmannanshire Field Studies Society, 1994

Jamieson, Drew. *The Ochil Hills - A Special Place.* (Second Edition). Amazon.co.uk, 2020.

Jamieson, Drew. *Fishing and Flying.* Amazon.co.uk, 2020

Thomas, Dylan. *Collected Poems 1934-1952.* J M Dent and Sons Ltd. London, 1952

Haliburton, Hugh. *Ochil Idylls and Other Poems,* 1891.

Steven, Kenneth. *Iona - Poems.* St Andrew Press. Edinburgh, 2000

Steven, Kenneth. *Salt and Light - Poems.* St Andrew Press. Edinburgh, 2007

Steven, Kenneth and Stewart, Wendy. *The Sound of Iona - Poetry and Music* (CD). Wild Goose Publications, Glasgow, 2018.

Kelsall, Robin. *Blairlogie Boyhood.* Self-published, 1999

Tullibody History Group. www.tullibodyhistorygroup.com

OTHER BOOKS IN THIS SERIES

"A Scottish Angler's Companions": "The author has met many people during a lifetime of angling but while most of us meet people, he befriends them and here remembers them fondly. Drew Jamieson …..shares that friendship with the reader in an easy to read manner.

"Where the Wild Trout Swim": "……written in a pleasant flowing language which is how all books should be written. I recommend it to all trout anglers but also to all lovers of the English language."

Tom McGregor, United Clyde Angling Improvement Association

"Trout from Scottish Reservoirs": "This is a fascinating read…… In many ways this book is a little gem, which provides both an historical account but also a reference for the management of trout reservoirs."

FISH Magazine, The Institute of Fisheries Management

"Where the Wild Salmon Run"; "A Scottish Angler's Companions": "Jamieson's writing evokes many different segments of the salmon's world…..He reaches far and wide to open a window on the history, culture, biology, science and joy of this wonderful wild animal. Jamieson's writing comes from the heart and it reveals a deep concern for the fish we love"

Atlantic Salmon Journal

"Where the Wild Trout Swim"; "Where the Wild Salmon Run"; "A Scottish Angler's Companions": "His careful observation of trout and salmon, his advice on managing reservoirs and the classic waters for anglers make these three books a great read. His charming boyhood tales and fishing experiences demonstrate his extensive knowledge."

Scottish Field

OTHER BOOKS IN THIS SERIES

- WHERE THE WILD SALMON RUN — Reflections of a Scottish angler — Drew Jamieson
- Fishing and Flying — A Homage to Terence Horsley — Drew Jamieson
- The Ochil Hills — A Special Place — Drew Jamieson
- WHERE THE WILD TROUT SWIM — Reflections of a Scottish Trout Angler — Drew Jamieson
- A SCOTTISH ANGLER'S COMPANIONS — Fly Fishing with the Masters — Drew Jamieson
- Trout from Scottish Reservoirs — A Valuable Recreational Resource — Drew Jamieson

by Drew Jamieson

Available on Amazon
amazon.co.uk

Notes

Printed in Poland
by Amazon Fulfillment
Poland Sp. z o.o., Wrocław